Really Reem

THE STARS OF

ESSEX

Becky Bowden

A Pillar Box Red Publication

Really Reem

THE STARS OF
ESSEX

A Pillar Box Red Publication

© 2011. Published by Pillar Box Red Publishing Ltd.

ISBN 978-1-907823-25-1

Images © bigpictures.co.uk

CONTENTS

A Little Slice of ESSEX
Where it all began

IT USED TO BE that only the most famous of film stars and the ridiculously rich were awarded a 'celebrity status' and given access to all of the high profile events in the entertainment industry. Times are steadily changing though and with an influx of reality TV shows hitting our screens it has become apparent that the British public and the media industry are definitely willing to embrace a generation of new young reality stars with open arms!

One of the hottest shows on TV right now has to be 'The Only Way is Essex'. With its mix of fun, entertaining personalities and exciting antics it has become a real firm favourite with many viewers who just can't get enough of anything and everything Essex related.

The BAFTA winning show, which first aired 10th October 2010 on ITV2 is based on a group of people who all live and work in Essex as the cameras follow their day to day lives. We follow a selection of fabulous people all from different walks of life and of various ages as they deal with the highs and lows of relationships, drama and love.

This regular programme has an ultra-cool, modern following and having produced three hit series so far it has seen the main cast members become household names and highly publicised rising stars on the celebrity scene.

We all know what the Essex guys and girls get up to on screen and we LOVE it but what do they do when they are not on camera? We bring you the stars of TOWIE doing what they do best as they attend glamorous events and star studded premiers. You'll see pictures of them out and about at some of the hottest venues as well as learning a little bit about each of

these really 'reem' personalities up close and personal in our mini biographies. Get all the info you could ever need on the stars who are beginning to merge together the world of TV and real life in the UK's answer to 'The Hills', 'Jersey Shore' and other well-known TV favourites.

Want to know which star studded event the girls of TOWIE were last papped at together? We have the low-down right here as we bring you Mark, Lauren, Kirk, Arg and co at their finest and don't worry there won't be a vajazzle in sight!

Essex Girls

The girls of *TOWIE* are very rarely seen without their best outfits, bronzed skin and perfectly primped and preened beauty regime. Each of these Essex favourites have been spotted out and about lately at various fancy locations, high profile events and not forgetting of course, the now infamous 'Sugar Hut' night club where the gang is often found on a local night out.

Find out which Essex girl was responsible for a whole new wave of 'vajazzling' trends and get all the latest info on our favourite Essex ladies, their super sexy style and all of the latest gossip surrounding their lives in the public eye.

What more could you ask for? Other than your very own Joey Essex of course, which unfortunately we can't deliver!

Essex Girl Amy Childs

AMY CHILDS has been a big part of TOWIE since it first began but after two successful series with the show she left to pursue other career options. Amy is funny, genuine and confident. She takes pride in her appearance and has worked as a beautician and a model in Brentwood, Essex.

Amy has gone from strength to strength in the public eye and her bubbly, fun personality seems to have struck a chord with TV viewers around the country, so much so that she was given her own regular fashion segment on ITV's hit show 'This Morning' where she looks perfectly comfortable and at ease in front of a camera, possibly thanks to all that experience on TOWIE.

She's a busy girl, with many strings to her bow. Amy was given a regular column in 'New!' magazine and can also add having posed for 'Vogue' to her list of achievements. This is definitely something that most young girls could only dream of having achieved at such an early stage in their career.

If that wasn't enough, Amy Childs also won National Reality TV Awards 'Best Personality of the Year' award in July 2011.

She made a shock appearance in 'Celebrity Big Brother 2011' on C5 and showed the public more of her real personality during her time on the show. She bonded well with everyone but undoubtedly seemed to click specifically with Lucien Laviscount, a fellow contestant and actor who has appeared in TV series such as 'Waterloo Road'. The pair denied any real romance and assured us that they were in fact just good friends. Amy gave the below quote to the 'Digital Spy' website in an open and honest interview after leaving the house: "He's a really good friend. There was so much banter between us and I always said we're both really young and he was the young boy in the house. We had such a laugh together but I seriously thought he was getting with Kerry. I seriously thought those two were going to be together.

"But Lucien is such a good friend to me and from this day on I'm going to be taking him to the Sugar Hut 100%, but nothing is going on between me and Lucien. It was just a bit of fun, banter, dancing – that was it."

Famous for her gifted Vajazzling ability on 'The Only Way is Essex', Amy is the ultimate beauty and style queen. She admits to spending hours on her makeup at times and is rarely seen without a great tan and a perfect pout. She loves to work her magic on others and was seen giving advice, tips and beauty treatments on both TOWIE and 'Celebrity Big Brother'.

Essex Girl Amy Childs

● ● ● ● ● ● ● ● ● ● ● ● ● ●

"nothing is going on between me and Lucien. It was just a bit of fun, banter, dancing – that was it."

● ● ● ● ● ● ● ● ● ● ● ● ● ●

Amy is not one to tell all about her social life and romance and we love her for that! She's had a much speculated on/off relationship with fellow Essex resident Kirk Norcross and has been quoted as saying: "We have always been on and off. There's loads of chemistry. But I don't know if I could have him as a boyfriend." When speaking to 'New!' magazine.

She's now signed to Can Associates Ltd management agency (yes, the very same one that has put pop superstar Peter Andre right back in the spotlight where he belongs) and we expect to see big things ahead in the future for this cheeky, down to earth Essex girl.

Essex Girl
Carol Wright

CAROL WRIGHT is mum to Jessica Wright and Mark Wright of TOWIE fame and also occasionally appears in the series herself. She is most famous for her repeated run-ins with Lauren (Mark's ex) as the couple faced regular family differences and a rather luke-warm reception to their on again off again romance. Speaking out about the couple's split, she said:

"It's a relief they've parted – they won't get back together and they shouldn't for their own happiness. They argued all the time and they were both so unhappy.'

"I still see Lauren when she needs someone to babysit their dog Wrighty and I'll always be here for her."

In a recent interview with 'Woman' magazine Carol went on to further reveal that her husband is considering a role on the show. Mark's dad has already been briefly spotted in a couple of episodes but Carol hints that this could turn into something more regular.

She said: "He put a lot of weight on over the years and I think that's what put him off. But he's been dieting and has already lost three stone. I think he's coming round to the idea."

You might be forgiven for thinking that Carol was often kept out of the loop with Mark's relationships but her comments reveal otherwise. This supportive mum says:

"I'm very close to my children and I know everything that they do, but there were times I'd be watching it and be thinking, 'God, who's Mark with now?' "

Hopefully we'll get to see more of Carol in the future as well as 'Big Mark' Mark Wright's dad, although I'm not sure they'll be joining the younger members of the family down at Sugar Hut any time soon!

Essex Girl
Chloe Sims

CHLOE SIMS is one of the newest TOWIE stars. She is famous for her positive attitude and stunning Jessica Rabbit like figure. She is the cousin of Essex boy Joey Essex and the two are very close, spending time together wherever possible.

She used to be a Playboy model in France and is familiar with life in front of the camera so fitting into the TOWIE crowd seemed to come naturally to her. She has made lots of great friends in the Essex area and is always spotted out and about at various nightclubs.

She likes to spend her free time travelling and recently took a trip to Vegas where she was pictured with none other than Paul Goss at one of his shows. The two got on really well and Chloe and her friends, The Pussycat Dolls founder Robin Antin and VegasBaby CEO Steve Littlechild, were invited back to his backstage VIP area, nicknamed 'The Gossy Room', where they tweeted pictures of themselves having a great laugh and striking a pose!

Chloe has spent much of the last few months playfully fending off the romantic advances of business man and nightclub

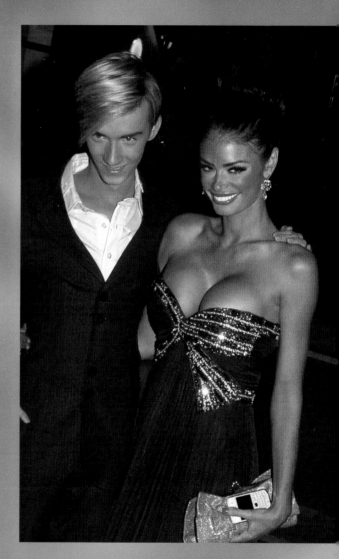

owner Mick Norcross and the two are just good friends now. You can't blame the guy for trying his luck though, who wouldn't want Chloe Sims on their arm?!

"I don't fancy Mick any more. I was in a weird state of mind before! He's a gentleman but the penny's dropped. I'm just not Mick's type."

Essex Girl Gemma Collins

GEMMA COLLINS came crashing onto TV screens during the first series of 'The Only Way is Essex' on ITV2. She was an instant hit with her outspoken and funny attitude and her general love for life.

She is friendly, bubbly and has an outrageous sense of humour. We love her for wearing her heart on her sleeve and for getting up to some very amusing antics on screen and in the public eye.

She is close friends with Kirk Norcross and developed a little (and by little we actually mean MASSIVE!) crush on his father Mick, although she insists she is over him. Gemma told the 'Daily Mail', "I don't fancy Mick any more. I was in a weird state of mind before! He's a gentleman but the penny's dropped. I'm just not Mick's type."

Gemma is definitely always up for a giggle. She donned her fortune telling gear and got her tarot deck out on Kirk's birthday to take up residence in the fortune telling tent, offering readings to party goers!

She is often spotted out at premiers and events but isn't quite as much in the public eye as some of her co-workers. She was recently spotted looking very glam at the Jeans for genes party in September though and everyone is bound to be looking forward to hopefully seeing more of Gemma in the coming months as this awesome 30-year-old rising star enjoys her new found fame.

Essex Girl
Jessica Wright . . . .

OUTSPOKEN, confident and sassy; Jessica Wright is a member of one of TOWIEs most high profile Essex families. The Wright Family (Jessica, Mark, Carol and the legendary Nanny Pat) have seen many ups and downs on the show and Jessica's life is just as fast paced when the cameras aren't rolling.

This multi-talented 25-year-old has enjoyed a successful modelling career as well as having worked as a furniture dealer and even as an eyelash technician. One of her mottos in life is "You only live once, but if you work it right, once is enough."

Jessica has a great passion for music and loves to sing. She used to be in a girl band called 'LOLA' (which stands for: Lovable, Outrageous, Loud, Ambitious) but has since decided to pursue a solo singing career. She was quoted as telling 'Heat' magazine the following in an exclusive interview:

"I'm back in the studio again working on my new music. I'm going solo now, it's definitely a more dancey sound than the stuff I was doing with Lola. I think it's going to be really cool."

You'd be forgiven for thinking that Jessica might be just a pretty face, but that certainly isn't the case. She has got a degree in Business & Marketing Management and is definitely not one to be taken for a fool.

Like all of her fellow Essex girl pals Jess is spotted out in public on a regular basis. A few of her favourite hangouts include the trendy 'Crazy Bear' restaurant in London, 'Zenna Bar' in London and of course the 'Sugar Hut' club in Essex which is now something of a local hotspot.

She recently celebrated her birthday at 'Aura' nightclub in London with fellow cast members and lots of close friends and family in attendance. Jessica arrived wearing a floaty white dress and looking like she was definitely ready to get into the party spirit!

A visit to Marbella is always on the cards on a regular basis for Jess and the girls, it is definitely their favourite place to holiday and there's plenty of sun, sand and fake tan on display in this fab holiday destination that seems to be just what the TOWIE gang love when they plan a getaway.

Jessica is often found spending time with friends soaking up the warmer climate in Marbella or 'Marbs' as the gang like to call it and is no stranger to being papped whilst lounging by the pool or enjoying drinks at the bar. It's an occupational hazard, but one which Jessica seems to be quickly learning comes with the job description! She's always only too happy to give a friendly smile and strike a pose and we love her for that.

"You only live once, but if you work it right, once is enough."

Jessica has attended a variety of different premiers, events and locations during her rise to celeb status and has been seen promoting everything from super-sized snacks at the 'Monster Munchies' premier with Matt Dawson and of course Nanny Pat, to launching the Ultimate dressing room in Malibutique in Birmingham.

She is a girl who knows where she's heading and how to get there and looks to be enjoying every step of her new found celebrity status. Rightly so!

Essex Girl
Lauren Goodger ●●●●●●●●●

Model, TOWIE star and on/off girlfriend of fellow Essex resident Mark Wright, Lauren Rose Goodger, born 19/09/1986, has found herself propelled into the world of celebrity stardom almost overnight since first appearing on 'The Only Way is Essex' on ITV2 in October 2010.

We think it's fair to say that her nine year romance with Mark Wright hasn't all been plain sailing! These two have gone from relationship bliss to rocky road breakup during its turbulent course of events and we suspect that there is surely more to come in this long running saga.

Lauren and Mark announced their shock engagement to friends and family during the second series of the ITV2 show and were met by a less than enthusiastic reaction from most, due to their previous track record.

The newly engaged Lauren gave the following comment in an interview with Mirror.co.uk regarding her thoughts on the public's perception of her and Mark's relationship:

"It's easy for people to get confused about who he's seeing and who he isn't," explains Lauren.

"But as far as I know, when he's been seeing these other girls, we've been broken up. I don't think Mark is a cheater. I think we have just broken up a lot. This is where people get confused. He's been single and people might not agree with it but he's a young lad and is going to try things out with other girls.

"Now we're back together and people think 'poor Lauren' that he's cheated. But actually he hasn't. I won't let him go and he won't let me go because we get on really well. We have great banter and we love all the same things. We're just right for each other."

Lauren and Mark have since seemed to have parted ways once again though, with

> ## *"We have great banter and we love all the same things."*

Mark posting the following on his official Twitter account in August 2011: "all who are asking i can confirm me and Luren have seperated. Thats all i can say now. She will always have a place in my heart."

Regardless of all her relationship drama with Mark, Lauren is a strong minded, outspoken individual with a great sense of humour. She is inspired by business savvy women and has set up her own official website where you can buy her official merchandise and 'Shop Lauren's Way' with a range of tanning and beauty products.

Favourite places to be seen include 'Quince' restaurant in Mayfair, London and the popular London 'Aqua' club.

Lauren has a pet Chihuahua called 'Wrighty' and she is often seen out walking him or proudly carrying him around. She is very family orientated and loves to spend her free time with friends and family relaxing or dancing the night away to her favourite singers: Beyoncé and Rihanna!

● ● ● ● ● ● ● ● ● ● ● ● ● ●

Essex Girl
Lauren Pope • • • • • • • • • •

LAUREN "POPEY" POPE was born on the 29th September 1983 and is a well-known face on 'The Only Way is Essex'. She's a DJ, model and an all round savvy entrepreneur who is probably currently best known to the general public for her time spent dating fellow TOWIE star Kirk Norcross.

The two have had an on/off relationship for several years and despite various arguments and break-ups they have kept returning to one another. Lauren once bought Kirk a super cute Bulldog puppy for his birthday and she has been at his side for many a public event and celebrity bash.

The road to romance is never smooth for these two however, as it was recently announced that they had decided to end their relationship once again. Whether the split will be permanent this time, we'll just have to wait and see!

> ## "We have great banter and we love all the same things."

Not content with working soley as a DJ, Lauren has branched into the world of music production and worked with rising UK singer Pierre White to remix his hit 'Broken' which reached no. 6 in the club charts. She is keen to release more of her own material and this girl is so determined we don't doubt that it will be a huge hit.

Entrepreneurial skills are another string to Popey's bow as she designed and launched her own range of clip-in hair extensions in 2007.

'Hair Rehab London' has been helped on its way by TV's favourite 'Dragon' Peter Jones, who after seeing Lauren show her product on his TV show series 'Tycoon' went on to help her launch the range, which is now stocked by celebrity hairdresser Alex Foden and continues to go from strength to strength!

Lauren has appeared in various music videos including 'Ready for the Weekend'

by Calvin Harris and has been named 'World's Sexiest DJ' by 'Nuts' magazine. She has performed at several celebrity parties and events and is no stranger to the club scene. She has reportedly spun for T-Pain, Neyo, Jenna Jameson and Lindsey Lohan. This event attracted a lot of controversy and press attention for her as it was around the time Lindsey was 'off' with girlfriend Sam Ronson.

Lauren is multi-talented and a definite triple threat in the entertainment industry. The girl is going to go far so keep your eye on her as she paves her own way to super stardom.

Essex Girl
Lucy Mecklenburgh....

LUCY MECKLENBURGH is one of the not so regular faces of TOWIE but when she does get air time, she certainly doesn't hold back! A fiery and confident young woman, Lucy never shies away from an argument and always makes sure that she puts her point across!

She's gone from being linked to Mark Wright, to having her own regular scenes. We look set to see more of Lucy in the future and possibly even her new love interest Mario Falcone, a bespoke tailor and designer.

Lucy and Mario haven't been an item long but they have already been pictured together on several occasions in the run up to the new series of the show. Mario is tanned, tall and hunky and the couple certainly look very cosy together whenever they are spotted!

> *"Being recognised is the best and worst part about the show."*

They were seen coming out of 'Alec's' restaurant together in Brentwood, Essex and were joined by Mario's mother. Meeting the parents already, it must be serious!

Lucy truly has her own unique fashion sense and knows how to work her style. Her long brunette hair is usually perfectly matched with a distinct air of 'rock chick' in her accessories choices. She was recently spotted wearing a floaty dress, paired with a black fitted leather jacket; something that fashion experts said just 'shouldn't' have worked but that somehow Lucy had managed to pull off without a hitch!

Lucy can often be seen out at various premiers and fashion and beauty launches. She is always perfectly preened, manicured and tanned and has appeared in various photoshoots for lads mags

such as 'Zoo' where she looked seriously smouldering with tussled hair and smokey eyes.

Speaking of her new found fame and the effect it has on her love life since becoming well known to the public and the press, she told 'Heat' magazine:

"Being recognised is the best and worst part about the show."

It looks as though Lucy is definitely no shrinking violet and that we should probably be prepared to see a lot more of her in the future! Bring it on!

Essex Girl
Lydia Bright

LYDIA BRIGHT first hit our screens on 'The Only Way is Essex' as the girlfriend of James 'Arg' Argent. The two have had their fair share of ups and downs during their relationship but always seem to end up together in the end! That's why we love them.

Lydia is a fashion conscious lady who loves to party and hang out with her girlfriends. She is often spotted out and about at the biggest and best nightclubs and confesses to often being the last one on the dance floor with her friends when they hit the town at the weekends.

Lydia told Mirror.co.uk:

"I'm ALWAYS the last one on the dance floor! Even if I don't mean to be, it's always me and my friend Chelsea, who's way worse than me. We will be the last two dancing until the lights come on, then we think, where should we go now? So we usually go and find some breakfast!"

You won't find Lydia curled up in front of The X Factor on weekends any time soon as she's definitely having far too much fun making the most of her exciting lifestyle and all that comes with being in the public eye.

> "*I'm ALWAYS the last one on the dance floor!*"

Like most women, Lydia loves to shop and most of her money undoubtedly ends up going on clothes. She was quick to snap up the famous Kate Middleton dress that went on sale at ASOS in June 2011 and wore it just days after, proving that she not only has great style taste but that she knows which looks are worth replicating on the fashion scene!

She hit London Fashion Week in style during 2011 and managed to get seated front row at the PPQ spring/summer 2012 fashion show. She was in great company surrounded by the likes of Peaches Geldof and Zara Martin. Go get em, gal!

● ● ● ● ● ● ● ● ● ● ● ● ● ● ●

Essex Girl
Maria Fowler

MARIA FOWLER is best friends with Lauren Pope and has had a number of high profile run-ins with Kirk Norcross. The two don't exactly see eye-to-eye on most things that's for sure and especially not where Lauren and Kirk's relationship is concerned.

Maria is loyal to her friends and loves a good night out with the girls. She is regularly spotted at Camden hotspot 'Gilgamesh' and other well-known clubs and restaurants.

Maria has made the move from UK glamour girl to TV personality, but has definitely kept her list of industry contacts well preserved. She is a regular on the London party scene and famously had a year-and-a-half-long relationship with F1 test driver Adam Khan which ended in March 2010.

She has been linked to Jack Tweed and Aston Merrygold and is a regular supporter of the Breakthrough Breast Cancer charity after her mother was diagnosed with the disease and subsequently beat it. Maria ran the Race for Life in 2010 alongside pal Kate Walsh.

We like her for her outspoken and carefree attitude and for the drama she brings to TOWIE! Keep it up, Maria!

Essex Girl
Nanny Pat

Nanny Pat Quotes

"You saucy git!"

"Ello Mark, I brought you some bread pudding!"

Talking to Mirror.co.uk about how her appearance on 'The Only Way is Essex' first came about: "They came to us and said they were doing 'The Hills' of Essex," recalls the unlikely celeb. "And Mark said, 'Nan we want you to be in it'. First I said no, and then I said I'd just do the one. You don't recognise yourself on the telly, I think to meself, 'Oooh – the way I'm talking!' A couple of people said, 'I bet you had to act' but I say no – it's easy, like."

Random fact

Nanny Pat once appeared as a judge on the 'Dancing on Ice' tour and was pictured with contestant and rapper Vanilla Ice backstage, tweeted by granddaughter Jessica later that day. She's certainly not afraid to embrace this new found fame!

To celebrate all things Nanny Pat, we've put together a quick-fire fact file on this cult TOWIE star who has gained herself quite a following. Who knows, maybe you'll learn a few pearls of wisdom from everyone's favourite Nan!

WHAT WOULD a book about our favourite Essex stars be, without a mention of the amazing Nanny Pat? Well known for baking her famous sausage plaits and of course for being Mark and Jessica's nan, we love this cheeky lady who definitely puts a smile on everyone's face with her hilarious antics.

Nanny Pat Fact File

Age: 75

Family: 5 children, 14 grandchildren and 6 great grandchildren. (Wow!)

Marital status: Widowed.

Likes: Baking, looking after her family, doting on her grandchildren and having a good old laugh.

Dislikes: Mark's attitude to women sometimes, peppery things and meatballs.

Essex Girl
Sam Faiers

SAM FAIERS is well known for her time on TOWIE as the gorgeous and confident girl who once had romantic ties with Mark Wright. She's now become a rising celebrity in her own right though and is often seen out and about with a whole host of famous faces at the biggest and best events and shows.

Sam definitely has the brains to go with the beauty; she's a business savvy chick with an eye for fashion. Sam and her sister Billie co-own Minnie's Boutique, a trendy and well known shop in Brentwood, Essex. Regular celebrity faces often pop their heads through the door to bag themselves a fancy outfit.

Jemma and Sam have become great friends, possibly due to moving in the same circles for various TV award ceremonies and events. They were also previously pictured in Manchester grabbing some dinner at a swanky restaurant and looking like they were having a good old gossip together!

Sam is passionate about fashion and so naturally, the clothing she stocks reflects this. She was spotted at London Fashion Week 2011 at the launch of 'House Of

Dereon' by Beyoncé and Tina Knowles, a range that she looks all set to bring to the rails at Minnie's as it goes from strength to strength! With front row seats to this popular show it is clear that Sam is becoming a force to be reckoned with on the fashion and media scene.

Sam had a brief relationship with fellow

> ## "I was mothering Joey – I just need space from him."

tour of where he grew up. This included such luxurious locations as the local dump! Erm, how thoughtful! We're sure he meant well though.

All seemed to be going well until Sam and Joey reportedly ended their relationship shortly before the third series aired. Sam writes a column for 'Star' magazine in which she filled her readers in on the relationship break down saying:

'I was mothering Joey – I just need space from him.

'He's gorgeous but we spent so much time together so quickly that the spark went out just as fast.'

So is there still hope for these two or will they move on just as fast as they hooked up? It looks unlikely with Sam having been spotted lately with a hunky new guy on her arm. The pair was first spotted together in the VIP area at V Festival in Chelmsford. New boyfriend 'TJ' has also been seen on holiday with Sam and her sister Billie in Ibiza, so who knows maybe we could have another really 'reem' relationship on our hands with a bit more sizzle than that of Sam and Joey! Only time will tell.

Essex co-star Joey Essex and the two were often spotted out and about together. They even went on a special 'glamping' trip with friends during one of TOWIEs brilliantly funny episodes and Joey treated her to a very special bike ride, taking in a

Essex Guys

The guys of **TOWIE** are no strangers to the spotlight. Frequently dazzling us with their bronzed bodies, their Essex accents and a cheeky smile, they've had us hooked since the very beginning.

As the guys' celebrity status grows they become increasingly well known in the public eye and can be found at all of the major star studded events. These lads are developing their own new identity and busy social lives outside of the show, proving that they are definitely a force to be reckoned with, in the dazzling lights of rising stardom.

With a splash of Mark, a hint of 'Arg' and a drop of Joey Essex stirred in for good measure you have the perfect recipe for guaranteed entertainment!

Keep reading to discover more about your favourite new faces of Essex with plenty of pictures and quotes along the way!

Essex Guy
Mark Wright

LADIES' MAN Mark Wright has had a history with many of the gorgeous women on 'The Only Way is Essex' including Sam Faiers and Lucy Mecklenburgh and he often causes a stir with his seemingly wandering eye!

Born on 20 January 1987, Mark's most highly publicised relationship was with Lauren Goodger. The couple got engaged during filming the second series of TOWIE after an on/off ten year relationship which ended on 26th August 2011.

Mark was once a semi-professional footballer with a youth career playing for Tottenham Hotspur, and Southend United, Grays Athletic, Rushden & Diamonds and Crawley Town. In September 2011, he joined non-league side Heybridge Swifts.

Mark's sister (Jessica Wright) Mother (Carol Wright) and Nan (Nanny Pat) also appear alongside him on your TV screens as they make up part of one of the most talked about families in Essex! He also has a brother Josh Wright who has yet to make an appearance on the show and is also a footballer. The skill must definitely run in the family!

He has a lot of celebrity friends; one of those being Jack Tweed, who he co-owns a bar with, but no-one comes close to the 'bromance' that he has with 'Arg' James Argent. The two are always pictured together and spend lots of time hanging out both on set and hitting the town.

Mark is really big on fitness and health and loves being at the gym, keeping himself toned and looking great. He takes a lot of pride in his appearance and although he works incredibly hard, he's no stranger to partying hard either. You can usually find him at one of the Essex or London clubs or holidaying in 'Marbs' or somewhere with equally as much sun, sea and sand!

Although he plays the tough man, most people who know Mark would probably tell you that he's actually got a heart of gold. He is very family orientated and his close friends mean everything to him. The world seems to be his oyster at the moment, and here's hoping he makes the most of it!

Essex Guy
Harry Derbidge

HARRY DERBIDGE is the cousin of reality star, ex TOWIE member and BB babe Amy Childs. The two can be regularly found spending time together at various beauty salons and both share a love for looking their best!

Harry often uses his catchphrase 'Shutttt-Uuuup!' and has become well known for repeatedly exclaiming the

phrase in various conversations with his Essex pals.

He was spotted on holiday soaking up the sun in September 2011 with Big Brother beauty Imogen Thomas and tweeted a picture of them posing by the pool. He's also no stranger to taking a trip to Marbella aka 'Marbs' and partying it up with the TOWIE gang.

He is a regular at 'Zenna' bar and 'Runway' nightclub in London and has been spotted at various celebrity events and screenings, including the 'Larry Crowne' world movie premier and the 'Fabulous Face and Body' opening in Harley Street, London.

His favourite wardrobe essential seems to be a cool, crisp white shirt and he's often seen pairing it with designer jeans and stylish shoes. He's confident, funny and completely random! That's what makes him adorable.

He has big plans for the future ahead and was quoted in 'New' magazine and the 'Daily Star' as saying:

"I'd love to do a duet with Chico. I went to his birthday party and he came to mine. We're bonding."

"I'm a dancer and I'm doing my own shows. I'd love to do 'Strictly Come Dancing' or 'Dancing On Ice'.

"But if anyone offered me a part on 'EastEnders' I'd do that too."

He added to the 'Daily Star': "I'd love to do a 'Glee' episode. I'd love Lady GaGa to come on the show."

So, pretty much up for anything then hey, Harry! Only time will tell as to whether any of these dreams will become a reality for the Essex star, but we think he'll definitely be exploring as many opportunities as he can during his time in the media spotlight.

Essex Guy
James 'Arg' Argent...

BORN ON 5th of December 1988 James Argent or 'Arg' as he is known to his friends grew up in Essex with parents Patricia and Martin Argent. He studied Drama, English Literature, Media Studies and Music at college and has won several well recognised awards including a 'Kenny Award' and a 'Judy Walker Award' for Best Young Actor.

Arg was a member of the Woodford Operatic and Dramatic Society. He played several roles including the Artful Dodger in 'Oliver' to Enjolras in 'Les Miserables' and Edmund in 'The Lion the Witch and The Wardrobe'.

He's a huge movie fan and loves to cosy up with a good film on a quiet night in and enjoys films like 'The Mighty Ducks' and 'The Karate Kid'.

Arg has been having a long term on/off relationship with fellow TOWIE star Lydia Rose Bright. The two have seen their fair share of ups and downs and experienced everything from Lydia being told by her girlfriends that they thought Arg may be cheating, to Lydia's hot date with a male model leaving Arg positively fuming.

Hopefully things will run a little more smoothly for these two during the next few

months as they could really do with a bit of happiness together!

Lydia isn't the only one who Arg is close to from the TOWIE gang. He is also best mates with Mark Wright. The two of them have one of the closest and funniest friendships ever seen and they always manage to raise a smile from those around them. It's a real modern day bromance!

Arg loves to indulge in his passion for singing and regularly performs at various shows and nightclubs. He has a soulful voice which doesn't do him any harm with the ladies that's for sure. You can expect to find him in one of the local Essex clubs of an evening (Sugar Hut, anyone?) or out with his fellow Essex friends in London's West End.

Loveable and fun, Arg is definitely a keeper! Hold on to your man, Lydia.

Essex Guy
Joey Essex

A REAL FAVOURITE with TOWIE fans, Joey Essex is a nightclub promoter from Essex who coined the word 'Reem' as his catchphrase. He wears super tight t-shirts and jeans, loves his Nike hi-tops and always wears his shoes two sizes too small, to avoid having 'clown feet'. Phew, if that isn't enough to make you love him, then what is?!

He has dated fellow Essex girl Sam Faiers and the two had been pictured together looking very much in love on several occasions. However, before the third series was due to air, the couple separated.

Joey has been busy releasing his own clothing line which is stocked in Selfridges none the less! The range of clothing will feature t-shirts with one of his classic lines "Look Reem, Smell Reem, Be Reem… Reem" plus a number of other well-known slogans and designs. We're sure it won't be long before the whole of the Sugar Hut gang are kitted out in this range for a night out!

Not content with stopping there, Joey has even got plans to release his own dance track. The single will feature his 'Reem' catchphrase alongside vocals from girl band 'Miss Millionaire' so listen out for it at a club near you and you could be dancing the night away to Joey Essex!

You have to admire Joey's enthusiasm and his eye for an earner. No doubt he'll soon be able to flash the cash at the hottest clubs and treat himself to a new pair of orange UGG boots with all of the money he'll be cashing in! Keep it up, Joey. You really are REEM and we love you for it!

"*Look Reem, Smell Reem, Be Reem...*"

Essex Guys
Kirk and Mick Norcross........

THIS FATHER and son team are regulars on 'The Only Way is Essex'. They are a very close family unit and Mick is always eager to spend time with his son, doing anything to make him happy.

He arranged a whole funfair to be set up for Kirk's birthday and invited all of his friends. Wouldn't you just love to have a dad like that?! The bash included classic fun fair rides, stalls and a fortune teller in the form of their mutual friend Gemma Collins.

Mick is often portrayed as a bit of a ladies' man and whilst he's not really in the public eye often enough to judge this for certain, we do remember a certain miss Gemma Collins having a mega crush on him!

Kirk Norcross works as a promoter for Sugar Hut, a nightclub in Brentwood, Essex. He has been involved in an on/off relationship with Lauren Pope, a DJ and a fellow TOWIE star. The couple have been

through various ups and downs in their relationship and Kirk just can't seem to make up his mind whether he wants to be with Lauren, or perhaps ex flame Amy Childs.

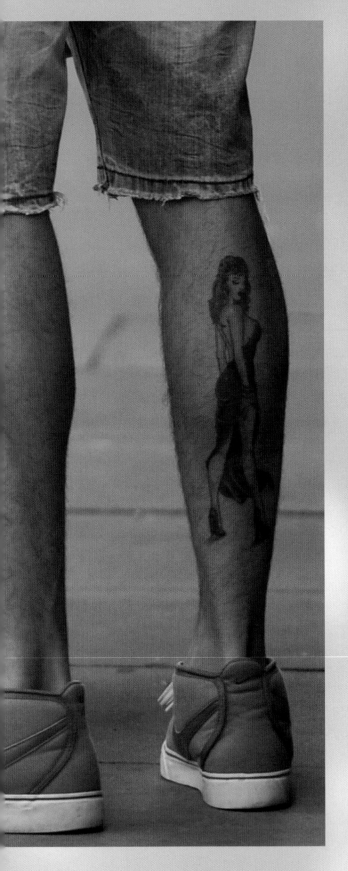

If I had to choose anyone to settle down with, it'd be her.

Kirk has regularly confessed to still having feelings for Amy, he even has a tattoo on his leg that looks remarkably like her! He told 'New!' magazine:

"I fancy her loads, I'd get back together as quick as that if I could. I'd settle down with Amy no problem. If I had to choose anyone to settle down with, it'd be her."

He insists that Amy is too busy with her work and career at the moment to rekindle their romance but we think that there could definitely be the potential for something happening between the two of them one day.

Kirk is a regular at various London and Essex nightclubs and loves to be out and about with his friends. He has attended several star studded premiers and has celeb pals such as Katie Price and her now ex-boyfriend Leandro Penna on his friends list! He was often spotted out and about with this celeb couple and was invited to her fancy dress birthday bash and on a trip to Thorpe Park.

When he isn't busy partying, Kirk shows his softer side by walking his pet Bulldog; a birthday gift from his now ex-girlfriend Lauren Pope. He was thrilled to receive this cuddly bundle of fun and it really is Kirk's pride and joy. Awww!

Essex Tweets

The Essex guys and girls could talk the hind legs off a donkey! These self-confessed chatterboxes are regularly posting social media updates and getting themselves quoted in magazines, check out some of their best quotes.

Gemma Collins

Good morning who's got the moves like jaggertoday? You can read all what I've been up to in my column today with closer magazine x enjoy xx

20th September 2011

Joey Essex

Filming for towie starts today! Woohoo excited mannnnn...
How is evryone this morning?

19th September 2011.

Joey Essex

Joey Essex Ken Doll! Who's buying one? Ha! :) I'm gona
bring mine round with me evrywere!

18 September 2011.

Chloe Sims

En route London baby!! Little Italy here come the girlsssss..
Frankies the BOSS Frankies the boss!!

16th September 2011

Chloe Sims

On my way to the TV choice awards tonight, hope towie
wins!!! Wish us luckk xxx

13th September 2011.

Jessica Wright

Gonna miss mum and dad tomorrow as they're away first time ever on my birthday... Suppose it was time I grew up! Got nanny pat with me xxxx

13th September 2011.

Jessica Wright

This weather is so depressing! Want to be in the Caribbean sippin on a cocktail watching the sun set... :-(

24th August 2011.

Jessica Wright

Twitter finally working again! Filming with the TOWIE crew for the advert - it's gonna be soooo funny can't wait for u all to see :-) xxxx

23rd August 2011.

Kirk Norcross

"Thanks for all the tweets guys! Yes me and Lauren have separated but are still pals!!! Love u guys! X"

17th September 2011.

Essex Tweets · · · · · · · · · · · · · ·

Maria Fowler

Nice to pop into TOWIE Towers n see everyone. Now driving home need food n pamperin back filming tomorrow! Xx

20th September 2011.

Maria Fowler

Just finished Closer Shoot now on way to Gatwick to eventually get to Dundee for a PA tonight! Hope to meet some of you lovely ppl there! Xx

14th September 2011.

Lucy Mecklenburgh

On way to the premier of 'Real Steal' it's got Hugh jackman as lead! Lovely! ..x

14th September 2011

Lucy Mecklenburgh

Alec's Restaurant with My Mario & his mum! X x

11th September 2011

Lauren Goodger

I'm goin 2breathe and smile!!Just makes u realise that u never really did no someone..! Anyway what's everyone doin 2day? The suns out yay x

13th September 2011.

Lauren Goodger

Go enue sorted for my bday party in couple weeks - ahhh so much 2 do such little time!! Shock I leave all 2 last min again ha x

12th September 2011.

Lauren Goodger

Just presented at the best high street fashion award! Having such a good night now I'm having few drinks with Lydia x x

8th September 2011.

Mark Wright

Finding love is very hard but getting over love is even harder !!

17th September 2011.

Essex Talk

• •

"When I'm with someone, I'm with them 100% – until then, I'll enjoy myself."

**Kirk Norcross
on the 'Daily Mail' website**

"I'm very comfortable with being famous," he told the magazine. "Life has changed incredibly – I'm doing photo shoots all the time and I get recognised a lot. Most of the time it's positive, but there have been negatives.

**Mark Wright speaking
in an Interview with
'Fabulous' magazine**

"I've had a brilliant time on *TOWIE* and loved every minute of it. I will really miss everyone. I so wanted to stay on, but I'm looking forward to what the future will bring and it's very exciting. I'd like to take this opportunity to thank all my loyal fans for their amazing support."

**Amy Childs in 'Glamour'
magazine on quitting 'The
Only Way is Essex'**

"My hair is looking reem"
"My shoes are looking reem"
"I'm looking reem"

**Joey Essex on
a Joey Essex Wiki**

Being 'Reem'
ESSEX STYLE!

So, we all know how to put on a bit of slap and get dolled up ready for a night out. If you're one of the *TOWIE* gang though, this might just take longer than you think! With a rigorous beauty regime and the desire to look really, really 'Reem' before they hit the town, here is what the gang might just be putting themselves through in order to look picture perfect for the next time you pick up your favourite glossy mag!

ESSEX STYLE!

The Tan!

It is ALL about the tan for the TOWIE guys and girls. Whether you are male or female, you need to get that perfect spray tan before even thinking about hitting the town for the night! Toned and tanned (occasionally verging more on the orange side if you get a bit trigger happy with the old tanning spray) every inch of you should be bronzed and beautified.

The Makeup!

Long, long lashes, smokey eyes and plenty of lip gloss to perfect that pout are an essential part of your makeover! Treat yourself to a manicure and pedicure to make sure that you look great from head to toe.

ESSEX STYLE!

The Fashion!

White stilettos may be the myth of Essex fashion days gone by, but apparently it's all about cream or nude stilettos nowadays if you're going to try and rock the latest killer Essex footwear trend! Playsuits, jumpsuits and wedges are also hot, hot, hot if you want to get a slice of this season's Essex style.

Statement accessories and cute bags (with a bit of bling!) always help to complete your look.

ESSEX STYLE!

ESSEX STYLE!

Guys' Fashion!

For the Essex guys it used to be all about wearing the lower than low, tight fitted v-neck t-shirts and skinny jeans to draw attention to your bod. Take note from Billie Faiers though who tells 'Fabulous' magazine that girls just don't find that look attractive anymore, they find it cringe-worthy!

ESSEX STYLE!

The Hair

Everyone should go red once according to sisters Sam and Billie Faiers, apparently it is 'big in Essex' so who are we to argue? Get rocking those red locks, pronto! Remember, if you get bored you can always head over to your local beauty boutique and get it changed back to your usual blonde or brunette look. Hair extensions are also favoured but not compulsory in achieving your Essex style.

ESSEX STYLE!

The Skin!

Exfoliate away the dead skin before applying lots and lots of your fave moisturiser, ready to soak up the huge amount of tan, makeup and primers that you are going to be applying later! No-one likes the flaky skin look and your tan just won't sit right, girls!

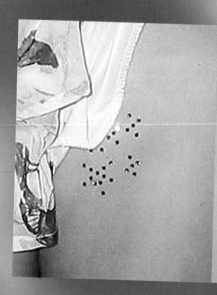

The Vajazzle!

After being a huge hit in TOWIE, the Vajazzle trend spread like wildfire across the UK. The art (if that's the right word!) of decorating your more intimate areas of your body with tiny adhesive crystals and gems was all the rage for girls looking to get in on the Essex fashion scene. You can even buy the DIY kits for home use now. Shut-Uuuupppp!

In the Spotlight

Your favourite Essex faces love nothing more than getting glam and heading out for a night on the town. Due to their new found celebrity status, some of them even find themselves invited to the hottest high profile events, clubs, parties and award ceremonies.

Here you bring you some of the hottest snaps of the **TOWIE** gang dressed in their glad rags and ready to pose for the paparazzi. Which of your favourites scrub up best?

In the Spotlight

'The Only Way is Essex' stars at 'Zenna' bar, London.

'Zenna' is a luxurious Indian themed bar in the heart of buzzing Soho. Locate the subtle entrance and descend steps lined with bronze water vessels of floating flowers and twinkling candles into the bar. Decorated with azure blue walls, soft leather and Oriental rugs, 'Zenna' is perfect for post-work drinks. Judging by the look on these lots faces, it's been a good night!

'The Only Way is Essex' cast on a fairground ride as part of Kirk's birthday celebrations, Essex, UK.

How did you celebrate your birthday? A party, maybe? Not Kirk Norcross, he went and created a whole funfair from scratch, just for himself and his mates! Now that's the kind of party to be proud of. Some familiar Essex faces are pictured enjoying the rides.

In the Spotlight

Lauren Goodger at Regis nail bar in Romford, UK.

Lauren Goodger was one of the celebs opening the N'OW @ Regis nail and brow bar at Debenhams in Romford, Essex. She looked pretty in pink as she signed autographs and helped on board at the event.

'The Only Way is Essex' cast enjoy the sun at a beach club in Marbella, Spain.

Marbs is the place to be, especially if you're a TOWIE regular. The guys and girls soak up some sun, sea and sand on a recent holiday to Marbella with everyone looking to be in high spirits.

In the Spotlight

Clothes Show Live 2010 at the NEC Birmingham, UK

See Mark Wright and Lauren Goodger get their glad rags on for the Clothes Show Live 2010 at the NEC in Birmingham. Is there anywhere that these two don't crop up? Looking good, guys!

Jessica Wright at the 'Save 4 Me' launch party in London, England

Jessica Wright was pictured attending the 'Save 4 Me' launch party in a stunning floaty iridescent sheer top. Apparently anyone who was anyone attended this star studded event. Jess certainly looked amazing as usual!

'The Only Way is Essex' star Jessica Wright seen out at 'Crazy Bear' in London

A real favourite for the TOWIE gang is the 'Crazy Bear' bar/restaurant in London. 'Crazy Bear' occupies two floors. In the basement delicious drinks are served up to a glamorous crowd resting themselves on swish cowhide barstools. Jessica looks to be having a great time!

In the Spotlight

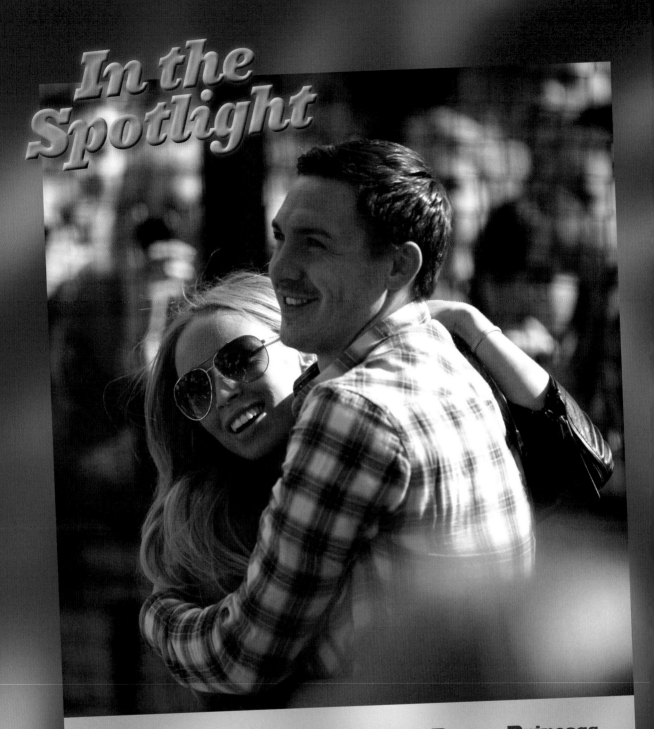

Katie Price aka Jordan, Leandro Penna, Princess, Junior, Lauren Pope and Kirk Norcross have a fun day out at Thorpe Park in Surrey, UK.

Lauren Pope and Kirk Norcross certainly mingle with some high profile celebrities! They were papped whilst enjoying a day out with Katie Price, Leandro Penna and family at Thorpe Park in Surrey!

Maria Fowler opens the new Sally Salon Services in Park Royal, London, UK.

The latest branch of Salon Services was opened in Park Royal recently with 'The Only Way is Essex' star, Maria Fowler, on hand to cut the ribbon. Wearing some killer Christian Louboutin Relika Patent Mary Jane Pumps and a dress that made sure she certainly wasn't going to fade into the background, Maria looked every inch the celeb.

In the Spotlight

The lovely Lauren Pope enjoying her 28th birthday celebrations at 'Zilli Fish' restaurant in central London!

Clutching a shiny balloon and surrounded by guests, this TOWIE star and successful DJ was dressed up to the nines to celebrate her special day.

The ever stylish Lydia Bright was spotted hot footing it around London.

There was no sign of her long term boyfriend Arg in tow, but she certainly looks cool and confident posing for a picture in a sleek black dress, silk scarf and her trademark bright red lips.

'The Only Way is Essex' star Gemma Collins was spotted out and about in a figure hugging white dress whilst getting the shopping in at Sainsbury's in Brentwood UK.

With her hair still in rollers and several bunches of dainty flowers in her hand, we can't help but wonder what this bubbly TOWIE star was on her way to get ready for!

In the Spotlight

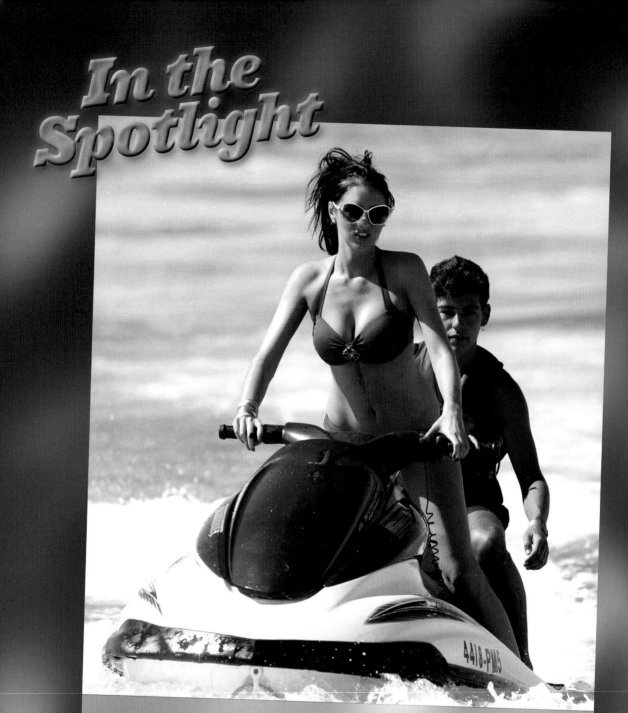

Amy Childs is spotted enjoying the sparkling blue sea in Portugal.

Dressed in a stunning blue bikini and a hot guy in tow, it seems that she was definitely having fun in the sun on her seemingly colour co-ordinated Jet Ski!

The Competition!

The guys and girls of TOWIE might be constantly in the spotlight right now, but let's not forget that they also have some serious competition from various other shows and rising celebs who also want a little slice of the elusive limelight.

The Competition! ....

SOME OF THE competition includes the cast of another well-known UK TV show: 'Made in Chelsea'. Although this rather more 'well to do' lot have quite different styles and backgrounds than our Essex faves, they are certainly hot on their trail and are spotted at star studded events and well known clubs more often by the day!

There have been several occasions where even the wardrobes of TOWIE and 'Made in Chelsea' have crossed paths, with two of

the girls snapped by the paparazzi in the very same outfit. Shock horror!

Lydia Bright from TOWIE was once spotted out walking her beloved Mr Darcy (her pet Micro Pig which are apparently all the rage right now) in the Essex countryside in a cute Laughing Cow t-shirt and then shortly afterwards Caggie Dunlop from 'Made in Chelsea'

The Competition!

was snapped wearing the same t-shirt, whilst taking a stroll in the sunshine along London's King's Road. Both girls are the leading fashionistas in each of their shows and looked equally gorgeous in their tees and micro denim shorts, but

fans will ultimately begin to question 'who wore it best' if occurrences like these keep happening!

The 'Made in Chelsea' cast which includes: Ollie Locke, Spencer Matthews, Fredrik Ferrier, Francis Boulle, Hugo Taylor,

The Competition! •••••••••••••

The new wave of Essex celebs are also constantly being compared to the stars of several US reality shows such as 'The Hills' featuring Lauren (L.C) Conrad, Spencer Pratt and Heidi Montag. This show swept the US off its feet, turning ordinary people into full blown celebrities overnight.

Milly Mackintosh, Amber Atherton, Alexandra Felstead, Francesca Hull, Rosie Fortescue, Caggie Dunlop and Gabriella Ellis are looking set to keep growing in popularity, especially given the fact that Chloe Green, daughter of the billionaire Topshop entrepreneur Phillip Green and girlfriend of cast member Ollie Locke has officially joined the cast of the show for Season 2. We sense rivalry both on and off screen for these rising stars, but keep it clean please folks. We love you all!

'The City' went on to have the same effect. The fantastic show starred everyone's favourite 'girl next door' Whitney Port, who became loved by the public for her series of down to earth comments and situations that people could really relate to. The scene where she fell on the stairs in a live segment of 'Good Morning America' had to have been one of her most endearing and embarrassing moments that made us remember that we were in fact watching someone's real life play out in front of the cameras and that nothing could ever be fully controlled or predicted, no matter how well edited!